The Best Book of The Moon

Ian Graham

KINGFISHER

NEW YORK

Contents

Author: Ian Graham
Managing editor: Sarah Milan
Series editor: Sue Nicholson
Art editor and cover design:
  Malcolm Parchment
Production controller: Kelly Johnson
Illustrators: Ray Grinaway,
  Roger Stewart
Photographs: John Frassanito and
  Associates/NASA (page 30)

KINGFISHER
Larousse Kingfisher Chambers Inc.
95 Madison Avenue
New York, New York 10016

First published in 1999

10 9 8 7 6 5 4 3 2 1
1TR/1298/WKT/MAR(MAR)/128KMA

Copyright © Kingfisher Publications Plc 1999

LIBRARY OF CONGRESS CATALOGING-IN-PUBLICATION DATA
Graham, Ian.
   The best book of the moon / Ian Graham.—1st ed.
      p. cm.
   Includes index.
   Summary: Examines the moon, its folklore, eclipses,
changing appearance, craters, mountains, exploration,
and effect on the tides.
   1. Moon—Juvenile literature. [1. Moon.] I. Title.
QB582.G7 1999
523.8—dc21 98-40377 CIP AC

ISBN 0-7534-5174-3

Printed in Hong Kong

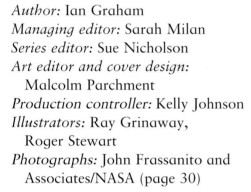

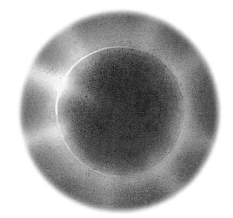

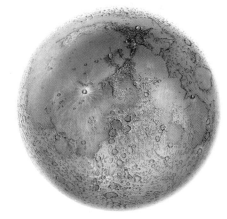

The magical Moon

In ancient times, many people worshiped the Moon as a god or goddess. The Ancient Romans called their moon goddess Luna. The Ancient Egyptians worshiped the moon god Khonsu. Other people did not believe the Moon was sacred, but still thought it had magical powers. Some believed that a full, round Moon could make wolves howl and make people go crazy, or "moonstruck." Today, most people do not believe the Moon has special powers, but they are still fascinated by its mysterious beauty.

Moon legends

In many countries, legends and folk stories tell of a man in the Moon, who was put there for stealing.

Other people see animal shapes, such as a cat, frog, or hare, in the markings on the Moon's face.

Moonwatching

Astronomers study the Moon through powerful telescopes. Some telescopes are built inside domes on top of high mountains. The domes protect the telescopes from the wind, rain, and snow. Far above car fumes, factory smoke, and bright city lights, the air is cleaner and clearer. This gives astronomers a better view of the night sky. You do not need a powerful telescope to study the Moon, however. You can learn a lot by simply watching it with the naked eye.

Daytime Moon

The Moon rises and sets like the Sun. You can sometimes see it in the sky during the day. However, it is harder to spot in the daytime because the Sun's light makes the sky very bright and the Moon seems to fade from view.

Moonwatching with the naked eye ...

... with binoculars ...

... and with a small telescope

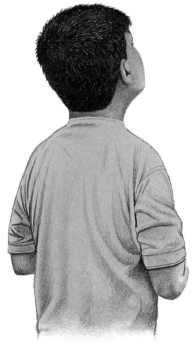

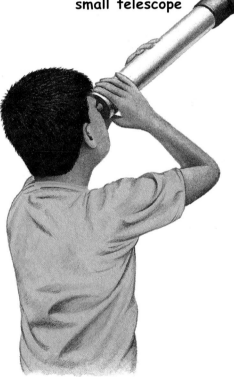

Naked eye

At night, it is easy to see the Moon with the naked eye. You can watch it change shape from night to night, and see patches of light and dark on its surface.

Binoculars

A pair of binoculars makes the Moon seem much bigger and closer than it really is. With binoculars, you can see mountains on the Moon, and hollows, called craters.

Telescope

A small telescope helps you discover even more. You can see hundreds of smaller craters, the walls of larger craters, and shadows cast by the Moon's mountains.

Mountaintop observatory

The Moon in space

The Moon is our closest neighbor in space, but it is still far, far away. It is the biggest thing we can see in the sky simply because it is much closer to us than anything else. The Moon seems to glow, but it doesn't give off any light of its own. We only see it because it reflects, or casts back, light shining on its surface from the Sun.

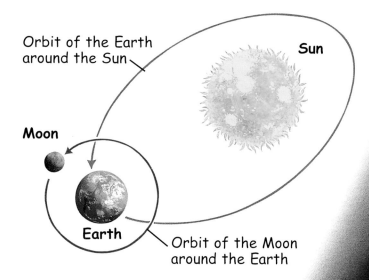

Orbit of the Earth around the Sun

Sun

Moon

Earth

Orbit of the Moon around the Earth

The Moon in motion

The Moon travels around the Earth and the Earth travels around the Sun in endless looping paths, called orbits.

Sun, Earth, and Moon
spinning through space

What we see

As the Moon orbits
the Earth, it keeps the
same side turned toward
the Earth. However, we only
see the parts of it that are lit
up by the Sun, so it looks as
if the Moon changes shape
from night to night.

Sun's light

Moon

Earth

Orbit of the Moon around the Earth

One quarter of the Moon's orbit of the Earth

New Moon
The sunlit part of the Moon is turned away from the Earth and the Moon looks dark.

Waxing Crescent
A day or so later, one thin edge of the Moon is lit up and we see a crescent.

First Quarter
After a week, the Moon has traveled one quarter of its orbit of Earth and we see a half Moon.

Waxing Gibbous
A few days later, we see more of the Moon's face, or a gibbous Moon.

Phases of the Moon

The changes in the shape of the Moon are called the phases of the Moon. The Moon changes from a new Moon to a full Moon and back again once every 29 and a half days, or lunar month. When the Moon looks as if it is growing bigger, we say it is waxing. When it seems to be shrinking, we say it is waning.

Moon festivals
In some countries in Asia, people celebrate the beauty of the Moon during the eighth lunar month, when it seems to be brighter than at any other time of the year. Children wear Moon masks and carry glowing lanterns.

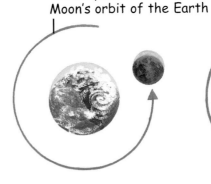
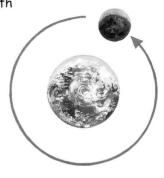

Full Moon

At full Moon, the Moon is halfway around its orbit and the Moon's whole face is lit.

Waning Gibbous

After a full Moon, the Moon begins to wane and we see less of its face.

Last Quarter

A week later, we see a half Moon again. The Moon starts the last quarter of its orbit.

Waning Crescent

As it completes its orbit, we see one thin edge of the Moon again.

The fall Moon festival in Vietnam

11

Eclipses

The Earth and the Moon cast long, dark shadows into space. Sometimes, as the Earth orbits the Sun, it passes between the Sun and the Moon. When this happens, it casts a dark shadow across the Moon's surface. This is known as an eclipse of the Moon, or a lunar eclipse. The Moon doesn't disappear, but turns a coppery color. When the Moon passes between the Earth and the Sun, it blocks out the Sun's light for a few minutes. This is called an eclipse of the Sun, or a solar eclipse.

Total solar eclipse

During a total solar eclipse, the Moon's shadow covers the Sun's whole face. The corona—the Sun's outer atmosphere—then lights up. Normally, we cannot see the corona because the Sun's light is so bright. Scientists travel from all over the world to observe a solar eclipse.

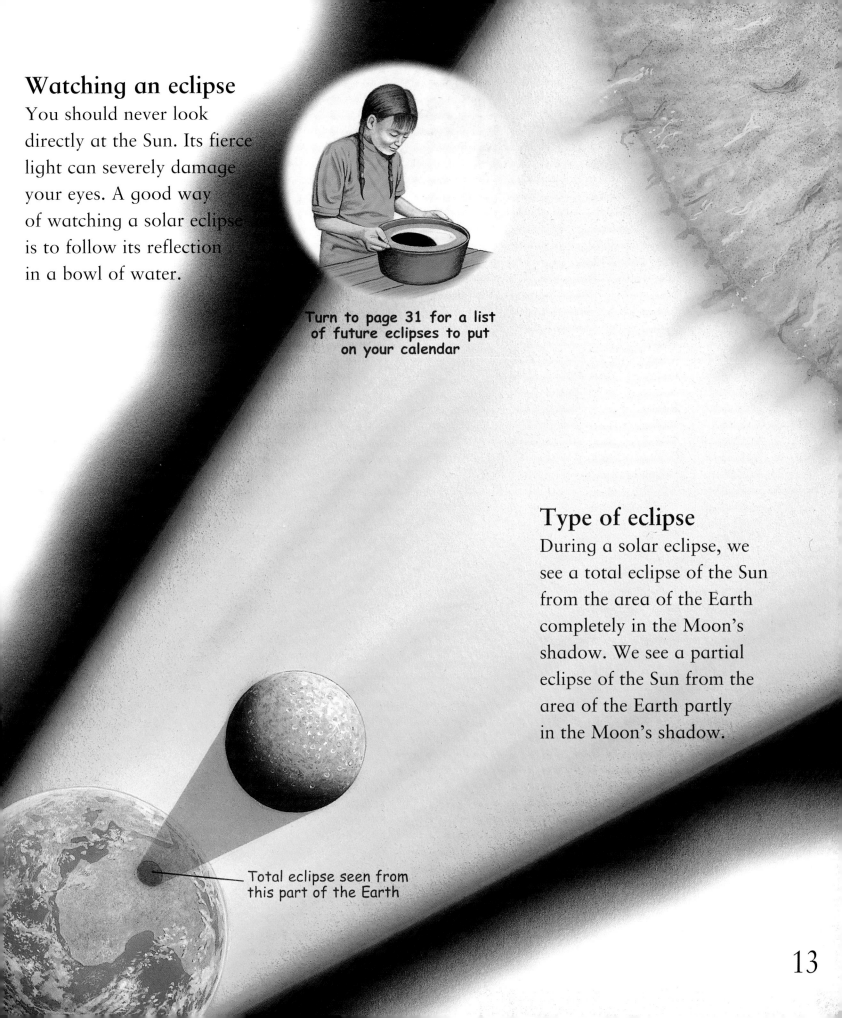

Watching an eclipse

You should never look directly at the Sun. Its fierce light can severely damage your eyes. A good way of watching a solar eclipse is to follow its reflection in a bowl of water.

Turn to page 31 for a list of future eclipses to put on your calendar

Type of eclipse

During a solar eclipse, we see a total eclipse of the Sun from the area of the Earth completely in the Moon's shadow. We see a partial eclipse of the Sun from the area of the Earth partly in the Moon's shadow.

Total eclipse seen from this part of the Earth

13

The Moon and tides

The oceans wash up onto the Earth's shores and fall back again twice every day. This movement of water, called the tides, is caused by the Moon's gravity pulling the ocean and the Earth toward it. The Moon's "pull" forms a bulge of water on the side of Earth nearest the Moon and another on the opposite side of the Earth. These bulges of water move around the Earth, following the Moon, and produce the tides.

First high tide

When the Moon is above this town, the sea is pulled up toward the land, producing the day's first high tide.

Spring and neap tides

At full and new Moon, the Moon and Sun line up with the Earth. The extra pull of gravity makes higher (spring) tides. In the Moon's first and third quarters, the Sun's pull lessens the Moon's pull and makes lower (neap) tides.

First low tide

As the Earth turns, the Moon's pull becomes weaker, so the sea level falls and gives the day's first low tide.

Second high tide

When the town is on the side of Earth opposite the Moon, the second bulge of water produces another high tide.

Second low tide

The tide ebbs (goes out) as the Earth continues to turn, and brings the day's second low tide.

Exploring the Moon

With the start of the Space Age in 1957, people began to learn more about the Moon. In 1959, a small space probe called Luna 2 became the first spacecraft to reach the Moon. Over the next ten years, dozens of different spacecraft circled the Moon, took photographs of it, and landed on its rocky surface. These unmanned space probes helped scientists find out whether it would be safe to send people to the Moon.

Surveyor 1 was the first spacecraft to land safely on the Moon

Safe landing

Seven Surveyor spacecraft were sent to the Moon. They showed that the Moon's surface was solid and safe to walk on.

Luna 2 was the first spacecraft to reach the Moon

The Eagle has landed

The famous words, "the Eagle has landed," were spoken by Neil Armstrong on July 20, 1969, when his Apollo spacecraft, nicknamed "the Eagle," landed on the Moon. A few hours later, he became the first person to walk on the Moon. Between 1969 and 1972, the Apollo space project landed twelve astronauts on the Moon in seven separate Moon missions.

Gemini spacecraft
Many of the maneuvers needed for a Moon landing had never been done before. Astronauts practiced in the tiny two-person spacecraft Gemini.

18

Apollo 14 Moon mission

Moonwalking

The Apollo astronauts walked on the Moon's surface for up to seven hours at a time. Each astronaut had to wear a space suit with a special backpack that supplied him with oxygen to breathe. The pull of gravity on the Moon is one-sixth lower than the pull of gravity on Earth. So although the suit and backpack weighed 178 pounds on Earth, they only weighed about 30 pounds on the Moon.

Scooping up rocks on the Apollo 17 Moon mission

Giant steps

Astronauts had to practice how to walk in the Moon's weak gravity.

They had to think a couple of steps ahead so that they could step or turn without difficulty.

Each stride also threw up clouds of fine dust which settled over the astronauts' legs and boots.

Moon gear

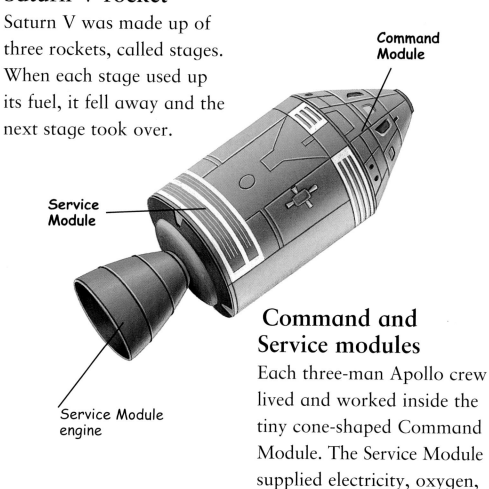

The Apollo spacecraft were launched into space by the world's biggest rocket, **Saturn V.** Saturn V stood 360 feet high and weighed around 3,000 tons. Most of this weight was the fuel needed to blast the 55-ton Apollo spacecraft to the Moon.

Saturn V rocket

Saturn V was made up of three rockets, called stages. When each stage used up its fuel, it fell away and the next stage took over.

Command and Service modules

Each three-man Apollo crew lived and worked inside the tiny cone-shaped Command Module. The Service Module supplied electricity, oxygen, and water.

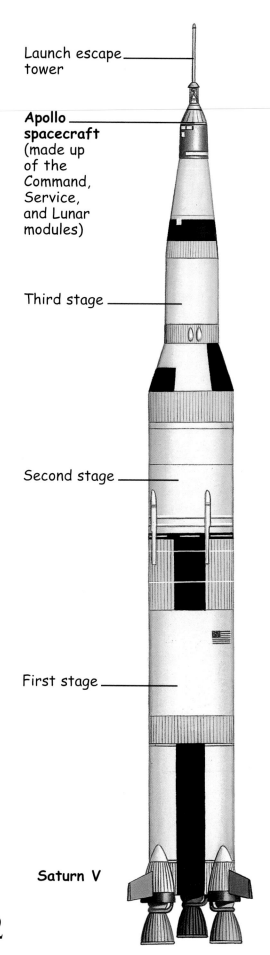

Launch escape tower

Apollo spacecraft (made up of the Command, Service, and Lunar modules)

Third stage

Second stage

First stage

Saturn V

Command Module

Service Module

Service Module engine

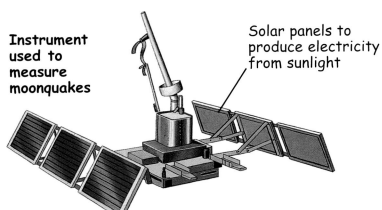

Instrument used to measure moonquakes

Solar panels to produce electricity from sunlight

Lunar Module

Moon experiments
Astronauts measured the Moon's temperature, detected moonquakes, and used a laser mirror to measure the exact distance between the Earth and the Moon.

Bottom part used as a platform to launch top part when leaving the Moon

Foot pads

Ladder

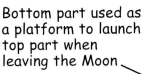

UNITED STATES

Lunar Module
The Lunar Module landed two astronauts on the Moon. The third astronaut stayed in orbit in the Command Module.

Dish antenna to carry astronaut's voice to Earth

Control panel

TV camera

Bags to hold rock samples

Moon buggy
On the last three missions, astronauts used a Lunar Roving Vehicle, or Moon buggy, so they could travel farther from the Lunar Module.

Wheels driven by electric motors which are powered by batteries

Collecting Moon rocks
The astronauts could not bend down in their space suits, so they used long-handled tools with scoops or claws at the end to pick up rocks.

Claw opens and closes

23

The face of the Moon

The same side of the Moon always faces the Earth, so the pattern of light and dark patches we can see on its surface never changes. The darkest patches are flat, low plains formed by vast flows of molten, or melted, rock that cooled and hardened millions of years ago. These plains are called *maria*, which means "seas," but they do not contain water. The lighter areas are craters, mountains, and rilles, or valleys. They are all covered in a dusty Moon rock called regolith.

Craters

Most of the Moon's surface is covered with thousands of craters, caused by rocks crashing into it from space.

Mountains

Mountains cover one sixth of the Moon's surface. These "highlands" are the oldest parts of the Moon.

Rilles

Rilles are long, narrow valleys, formed by cracks in the Moon's crust or carved out by rivers of lava.

Moon rocks

Breccia

Basalt

Holes made by gas escaping when the rock was molten

Anorthosite

Moon history

Moon rocks and soil samples collected by astronauts have provided scientists with important clues about the Moon's history. Tests showed that the Moon's rocks are similar to rocks found all over the Earth. Because of this, scientists now think that the Moon may once have been part of the Earth.

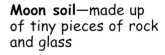

Moon soil—made up of tiny pieces of rock and glass

Birth of the Moon

1

1 Some scientists believe the Moon was formed about four billion years ago, when the Earth was hit by a piece of rock as big as the planet Mars.

2 The collision blasted a huge amount of rock from Earth out into space. The shattered pieces of rock went into orbit around the Earth.

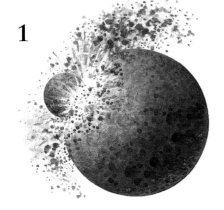

2

3

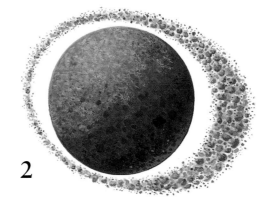

3 Over millions of years, the rocks clumped together to form the Moon. Molten lava gushed up onto the surface from deep inside, making the *maria*, or seas.

How a crater is formed

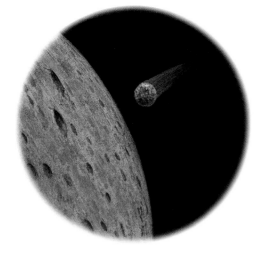

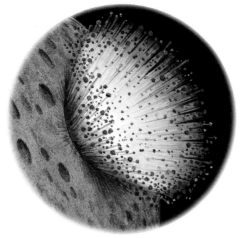

1 Most of the Moon's craters were made by asteroids, or space rocks, crashing into the seas or the middle of older craters.

2 Fierce heat made by the collision destroyed the original asteroid, and shattered and melted the surrounding Moon rock.

3 Rock and dust flung up into space settled around a bowl-shaped crater. Some Moon craters are hundreds of miles wide.

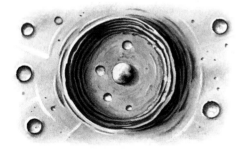

Terraced crater

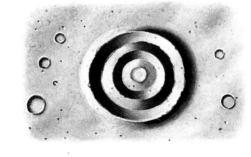

Concentric crater

Ray crater

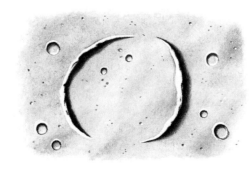

Ghost crater

Moon craters

Most Moon craters are simple bowl-shaped hollows with low rims. Others have steep, terraced sides with hills or mountains in the middle. Concentric craters look like rings inside rings. They may once have been volcanoes. Ray craters are surrounded by gray streaks, or rays, made by lighter colored rocks. Older ghost craters have been almost filled in by molten rock.

Moon maps

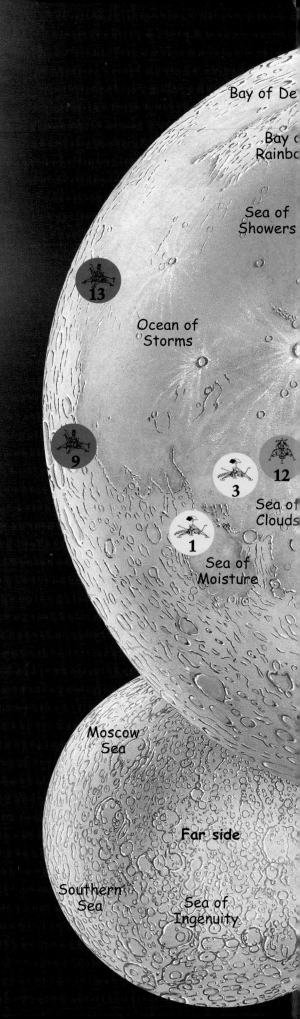

Bay of De

Bay of
Rainbo

Sea of
Showers

Early maps drawn by astronomers 400 years ago did not show all the Moon's craters and seas. This was because their telescopes were not very powerful. More detailed maps were made as telescopes became stronger. The most accurate Moon maps were made using photographs taken by space probes in the 1960s.

13

Ocean of
Storms

9

3

12

Sea of
Clouds

1

Sea of
Moisture

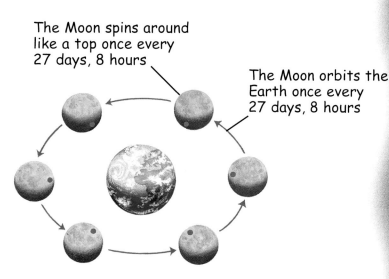

The Moon spins around like a top once every 27 days, 8 hours

The Moon orbits the Earth once every 27 days, 8 hours

Moscow
Sea

Far side

Why we see one side

The Moon takes the same length of time to rotate once as it does to travel all the way around the Earth. This means that the same side of the Moon always faces the Earth.

Southern
Sea

Sea of
Ingenuity

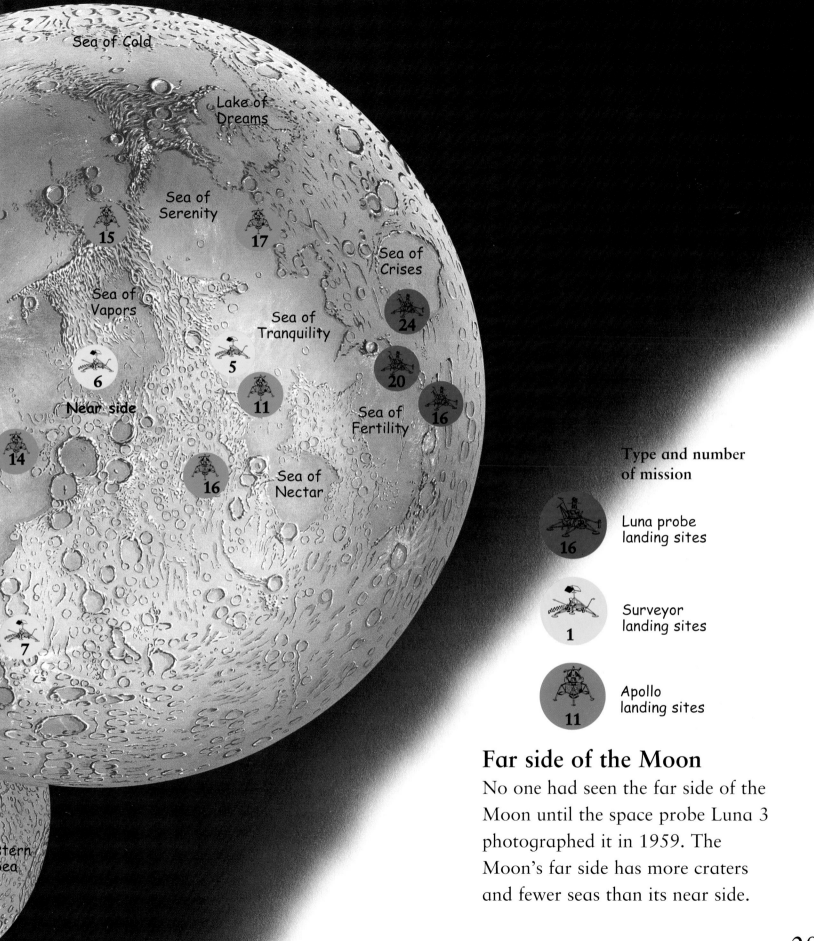

Sea of Cold

Lake of Dreams

Sea of Serenity

15

17

Sea of Crises

Sea of Vapors

24

Sea of Tranquility

5

6

20

Near side

11

16

14

Sea of Fertility

16

Sea of Nectar

7

stern ea

Type and number of mission

16
Luna probe landing sites

1
Surveyor landing sites

11
Apollo landing sites

Far side of the Moon

No one had seen the far side of the Moon until the space probe Luna 3 photographed it in 1959. The Moon's far side has more craters and fewer seas than its near side.

29

Moonbases

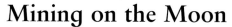

In the future, people may travel to the Moon to live and work. We may dig valuable minerals out of the Moon's rocks. Astronomers would like to build telescopes on the far side of the Moon, where they would have a fantastic view of the stars. We may build giant spacecraft in orbit around the Moon in order to carry astronauts to distant planets.

Prospector probe

In 1998, the Prospector probe found water frozen in rocks on the Moon. This could be used to supply moonbases.

Mining on the Moon

Valuable minerals could be mined on the Moon and sent back to Earth. Moon miners would live on a specially built moonbase and wear space suits to go to work.

Delivering oxygen plant

Building oxygen plant

Building living quarters

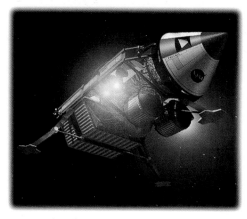

Arrival of crew

Living and working on the Moon

Glossary

antenna A length of wire, a metal frame, or a dish-shaped sheet of metal used to send or receive radio signals.

Apollo American space project that landed astronauts on the Moon.

basalt Volcanic rock made from hardened lava; the most common rock on the Earth and the Moon.

breccia Rock made from soil and rock squeezed together when hit by a falling object.

corona The Sun's atmosphere, only visible during a solar eclipse.

gibbous Looking bigger than half a circle but smaller than a whole circle.

maria Latin word meaning seas; used by early astronomers for the dark patches on the Moon's surface which they thought may contain water.

module One complete part, or section, of a spacecraft.

molten Melted; molten rock is also called lava.

orbit The endless path of a spacecraft around the Moon, the Moon around the Earth, or any planet around the Sun.

oxygen A gas with no color or smell. We need oxygen to breathe in order to live.

rille A long, thin valley on the Moon carved out by flowing lava.

Sea of Tranquility The part of the Moon where the first astronauts landed in July 1969.

Space Age The time since October 4, 1957, when the first artificial satellite, Sputnik 1, was launched into space around the Earth.

tide The twice daily movement of the sea up onto the shore and down again caused by the pull of the Moon's gravity.

waning Seeming to grow smaller.

waxing Seeming to grow larger.

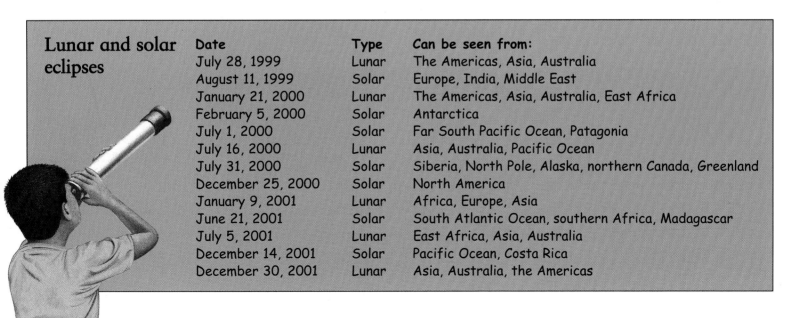

Lunar and solar eclipses	Date	Type	Can be seen from:
	July 28, 1999	Lunar	The Americas, Asia, Australia
	August 11, 1999	Solar	Europe, India, Middle East
	January 21, 2000	Lunar	The Americas, Asia, Australia, East Africa
	February 5, 2000	Solar	Antarctica
	July 1, 2000	Solar	Far South Pacific Ocean, Patagonia
	July 16, 2000	Lunar	Asia, Australia, Pacific Ocean
	July 31, 2000	Solar	Siberia, North Pole, Alaska, northern Canada, Greenland
	December 25, 2000	Solar	North America
	January 9, 2001	Lunar	Africa, Europe, Asia
	June 21, 2001	Solar	South Atlantic Ocean, southern Africa, Madagascar
	July 5, 2001	Lunar	East Africa, Asia, Australia
	December 14, 2001	Solar	Pacific Ocean, Costa Rica
	December 30, 2001	Lunar	Asia, Australia, the Americas

Index